Gladis María Demarchi

Tips for the Presentation

of a Good Project

Evaluation Proposal

Data to include when applying as

external consultants for contracts with

international organizations.

Gladis María Demarchi

Biography:

Gladis María Demarchi: Bachelor in International Relations and Master in Latin American Social and Political Studies with extensive experience working as an international consultant.

Specialist in planning, design, monitoring and evaluation of public policies, programs and social projects developed in Latin America according to the results-based management model, methodologies and other tools used by international organizations.

Expert in systematization of information and interpretation of data from primary and secondary sources.

Mentor of emerging evaluators.

Tips for the Presentation of a Good Project Evaluation Proposal

Links to contact the author:

gladis.demarchi@outlook.cl

About this book:

This book is intended to be a simple guide with practical advice for those consultants who wish to present a good project evaluation proposal.

First, what led me to prepare this guide is the little information that is available mainly to young or less experienced evaluators when they wish to participate in the various selection processes as external consultants to contracts of international organizations.

Although each organization has its own requirements, there are some data that are always necessary to provide when presenting a good technical and financial proposal in a concise and summarized manner.

For this reason, this guide provides recommendations and indicates in a practical way all the information required to apply and be selected as independent evaluators.

Do you want to know what those tips are?

Gladis María Demarchi

Acknowledgements:

I would like to thank all my professors and tutors in the various instances of studies I have pursued throughout my life.

To life, for giving me this opportunity to share my practical knowledge with the younger consultants who are just entering the project evaluation area.

Thank you very much.

I would like to express my appreciation to Nadine Lorena Sperduti for the translation of this book from the Spanish to English language.

Dedication:

This book is dedicated to all those individuals who have given their lives or give their time to ensure human rights internationally.

To all international organizations that seek to ensure the fulfillment of rights in general by calling for independent assessments of the development projects they have implemented.

Gladis María Demarchi

Smart Book:

This book includes QR codes that will direct readers to different links with references and/or contact sites.

All this was done in order to enable greater interaction with readers and provide a space for communication between them and the author.

Over time, the intention is to incorporate more templates, graphics, diagrams, and other practical tips.

ISBN: 9798495287594

Gladis María Demarchi

Tips for the Presentation of a Good Project Evaluation Proposal

Tabla de contenidos:

.

Tips for the Presentation of a Good Project Evaluation Proposal

Data to include when applying as external consultants for contracts with international organizations.

Gladis María Demarchi

Gladis María Demarchi

TEN PRACTICAL TIPS FOR APPLYING FOR PROJECT EVALUATIONS

The requirements to be met in the selection processes for external consultants described in the Terms of Reference (TOR)[1] published by international organizations are often quite difficult to understand, especially for younger evaluators or those who are just starting their professional career in this field.

To this must be added the fact that most organizations request the inclusion of a technical-financial proposal in which the approach, methodology and work plan to be followed must be clearly described in a maximum of five to seven pages.

This is to ensure that the applicant has understood the type of evaluation required and that all the procedures will be followed to verify compliance with certain indicators towards the achievement of the project's objectives according to the results-based management model, as well as its alignment with international development objectives.

---

[1] Terms of Reference: document prepared by an international organization for the purpose of contracting consultants and/or external companies to provide certain services.

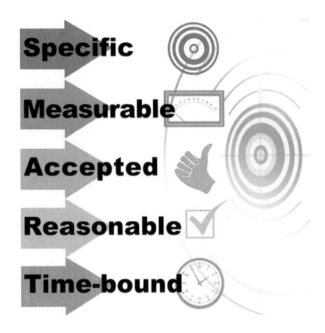

In general, the TORs not only describe the background of the project with its expected results matrix, but also indicate the need for the applicant as evaluator to fill out a series of documents presented as annexes following a specific format.

Frequently, it is necessary to include a letter of interest, a curriculum vitae in a specific form, a technical and financial proposal, simple affidavits, a declaration of beneficiaries, among others.

Undoubtedly, for an evaluator without much experience in such processes, the most complex task is the preparation of a technical and financial proposal so as not to be discarded in the first round of selection.

But before elaborating such a methodological proposal, I would like to point out some ten useful tips for participating in such processes, which are mentioned below:

1. First, when getting to know the ToRs it is very important to quickly check if the applicant meets, at least, the minimum requirements to be considered in the selection process such as age, nationality, number of years of experience, etc. In addition, check the desirable requirements to be met to see if the applicant's experience matches the specific skills requested.

2. Carefully read the ToRs to see the type of contract being offered and the time required to fulfill the consultancy.

3. Verify the work conditions required such as whether the work will be performed remotely or will include mission travel. [2]

4. See what type of evaluation will be carried out, for example, whether it is formative or summative, intermediate, or final, because the objectives to be achieved will depend on the nature of the evaluation.

5. Examine the necessary documentation to be submitted according to the accompanying annexes and the required form.

6. Begin to complete said documentation according to the project background provided in the ToRs, the results framework matrix, the logical framework matrix, the theory of change model, etc.

7. If a description of the methodology and approach to be followed is required, prepare a clear and concise technical and/or financial proposal. This topic will be discussed in more detail and in greater depth later.

8. Proceed to sign the documentation on which it explicitly states that it must bear full name, date and signature.

9. In case the application must be made online, upload the documentation to be sent to the specified site in the format detailed according to the number of files indicated with the weight accepted for this purpose. On the other hand, if it

---

[2] Some cases may include destinations in conflict areas, special visa requirements or one or more vaccinations.

must be sent by e-mail, indicate in the subject line the reference name of the project to which the selection process refers and in the body of the e-mail indicate the addressee, describe in three to five lines the purpose of the e-mail, attach the documentation, and say goodbye with a formal and polite greeting.

10. Send the e-mail requesting, as far as possible, a response of its correct reception and then make sure that it is not returned due to typing errors in the e-mail address, excessive weight of files and automatic responses.

METHODOLOGICAL PROPOSAL

<u>TECHNICAL PROPOSAL:</u>

Context

First, describe in the context paragraph the agency implementing the project, indicating its full name together with the reference number by which it is identified, the local and temporal scope of the evaluation in no more than ten lines.

Also, indicate the type of evaluation to be carried out, whether it is a mid-term or final review, formative or summative, etc. This is very important since the objectives will depend on the nature of the evaluation to be carried out.

Evaluation Objectives and Purpose

Describe the **general objective** of the evaluation, which usually appears in the ToRs and is related to the measurement of project performance, the achievement of project objectives and the attainment of superior project results.

Depending on the type of evaluation, it is very usual to try to comply as best as possible, at least, with the following criteria[3]:

- Relevance: this refers to the extent to which the project and its expected results or outputs are consistent with national and local policies and priorities, partners, and beneficiaries' needs.

- Coherence: the compatibility of an initiative with other interventions in a country, sector, or institution.

- Efficacy: is the degree to which project outputs and outcomes have been achieved or the extent to which progress has been made toward planned outputs and outcomes. The difference between efficacy and effectiveness is that the latter measures the ability to fulfill achievements at the practical level.

- Efficiency: is the ratio of resources or inputs over the time required to achieve the established outcomes and outputs; the

---

[3] In Better Criteria for Better Assessment: Revised definitions of assessment criteria and principles for their use by the Organization for Economic Co-operation and Development, (OECD), 2019, https://www.oecd.org/development/evaluation/Criterios-evaluacion-ES.pdf

quality of the outputs delivered; country ownership; stakeholder participation; financial planning; the performance of national agencies and the designated oversight agency; the coordination mechanism with other projects and programs; the reasons for delays in the delivery of project outcomes and outputs; and other factors and processes that affect the achievement of project results.

- Sustainability: analyzes the likelihood of sustainable results at project completion; the availability of financial resources; the socio-political environment; the catalytic or multiplier effects of the project; and institutional, governance and environmental risks.

- Impact: verifies the extent to which the project has contributed or is likely to contribute to intermediate states toward the intended impact, such as changes in the behavior of stakeholders or its impact on the lives of beneficiaries and the environment.

In addition, it is possible that efforts will be made to measure some facilitating elements; the logic of the design; the limitations found in their final scope; the mitigation measures for problems detected; the installed capacity; the functioning of the monitoring and evaluation system; some lessons learned; and recommendations for their replicability or scaling up.

In the **specific objectives:**

Include all the objectives described in the ToRs themselves and in case they are not mentioned in them detail more precisely all the criteria and other factors that the review intends to measure.

In general, it is requested to evaluate the following:

- ✓ Provide findings on the degree of relevance, coherence, effectiveness, efficiency, sustainability, and impact.
- ✓ Assess compliance with the project's superior results and objectives considering the positive and negative effects generated.

16

✓ Evaluate whether the gender equality approach has been mainstreamed, whether free, prior, and informed consent (FPIC) has been applied in the case of implementation in areas or neighboring zones with the presence of indigenous peoples, and compliance with human rights in general.

✓ Analyze the critical points and difficulties encountered in the project implementation processes; the mitigation measures adopted; extract lessons learned, and some good practices detected.

✓ Identify actions necessary for the appropriation and sustainability of the results.

✓ Propose or determine the possibility of replicating or scaling up the project.

As already mentioned, these objectives will depend on the type of review to be carried out.

Regarding the **purpose** of the evaluation, in general, it is customary to request the verification of the performance achieved by the project; the identification of unforeseen results in order to be able to take mitigation measures and make a projection for sustainability strategies of the results; the recovery of lessons learned; and accountability to donors, among other activities.

The following is a description of the minimum questions considered in the ToRs for each proposed evaluation criterion, as well as the

17

inclusion of cross-cutting issues such as gender equity, human rights, participation of local communities, indigenous peoples and affected minorities.

It should be noted that when preparing the Evaluation Matrix for the Inception Report it will be determined whether it is necessary to add other questions such as the alignment of the project with the Sustainable Development Goals[4] and the degree of collaboration with other national and regional initiatives.

---

[4] Sustainable Development Goals, United Nations, 2012:
https://www.un.org/sustainabledevelopment/es/objetivos-de-desarrollo-sostenible/

Methodology

In the description of the methodology, indicate the regulatory assessment frameworks to be taken into account and the analysis approach to be followed.

Given that each organization tries to comply with the principles of one or several regulatory frameworks, name each of them and paste the respective links in the text or put them as footnotes if there are several.[5]

Include a table with the Evaluation Matrix to be used, trying to ensure an adequate balance between quantitative and qualitative indicators. (Annex 1)

Describe the analysis approach to be used which, in most cases, is based on the Theory of Change Model. The purpose of using such an approach is to focus on the review of outputs and outcomes in order to determine the achievement of the various higher project objectives while taking into account the influence of external factors that may have had an effect on the achievement of these outcomes.

---

[5] Ethical Guidelines for Evaluation, United Nations Evaluation Group, UNEG, 2020: http://www.unevaluation.org/document/detail/2866

Based on the project background and the Project Results Framework, a simplified model of analysis can be developed to ensure that the applicant has a thorough understanding of what is being evaluated.

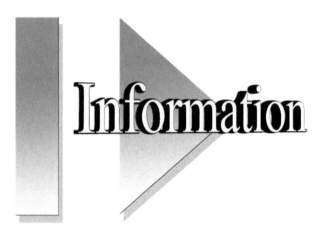

For more information about the Theory of Change scheme you can review the following QR code:

Data collection:

It is important to mention that, to determine the fulfillment of outputs, outcomes and the possible level of impact, an attempt will be made to inquire to what extent the project interventions have contributed to the achievement of higher-level outcomes.

For this purpose, both primary and secondary sources will be considered:

Secondary sources:

Indicate that a review of project documentation will be carried out and cite first those highlighted in the ToRs and any others considered relevant according to the type of evaluation:

- Project document.
- Evaluation regulatory framework.
- Annual work plans.
- Semiannual and annual reports.
- Interim reviews in case a final evaluation is being applied for final evaluation.
- Technical-financial and expenditure reports.
- Reports to the donor.
- Minutes of project committee or board meetings.

- Budget revisions.

- Legal documents.

- Technical reports, products, and consultancies.

- Web sites.

- Add that the consultants, if necessary, may request other documentation during the review such as publication campaigns, brochures, videos, training attendance lists, etc.

Primary Sources:

In general, tenders usually indicate data collection methods including interviews, surveys, focus groups, field visits, etc.

Detail all those that are deemed convenient considering the duration of the consultancy, the work team, the time required for data analysis and interpretation, and the mobility conditions for data collection.

The idea is to ensure a balance between qualitative and quantitative data collection.

For this purpose, the following collection methodology can be proposed:

(a) Semi-structured interviews: individual or group, face-to-face or virtual through Zoom, Microsoft Teams, Google Meet, Skype, WhatsApp, and telephone interviews with key informants, including government parties; country and regional agency staff involved in the project; representatives of other bilateral or multilateral initiatives that have participated; consultants; academia; civil society organizations; beneficiaries and representatives of local communities, among others.

b) Surveys and questionnaires: face-to-face or online using, for example, Google forms for a specific topic and, if available, e-mail or contact information of the potential persons to be consulted.

c) Discussion groups: these can be made up of trained personnel, beneficiaries, and non-beneficiaries in order to deal with a specific topic and to know the opinion of those affected by the project. If they are face-to-face, groups of no more than seven to ten participants can be formed, and if they are conducted virtually, they can be made up of three to five members.

d) If possible, propose a couple of field visits to make a direct observation of pilots, business models, etc.

If the visit is not feasible in order to verify the level of progress achieved by the project, the beneficiaries may be asked to take video photographs or virtual tours during the interview.

It should be noted that gender parity, human rights and the Sustainable Development Goals will be taken into account at all times.

Analysis techniques:

Ensure the use of mixed methods (quantitative and qualitative) and triangulation of information in all instances for verification of conclusions:

- Quantitative analysis method: review of disaggregated data, as far as possible, considering differences by age, sex, ethnicity, rural or urban area, socio-economic level, educational level, etc. with special emphasis on cross-cutting issues such as gender equity, human rights, indigenous communities, and minorities.

- Qualitative analysis method: using the information obtained from interviews, focus groups, field visits or virtual tours.

Always ensure a respectful and transparent approach to the internal and external parties consulted.

Deliverable Products

Describe the expected deliverables of the consultancy with their respective deadlines and minimum or maximum number of pages indicated in each case.

Inception Report: include the evaluation matrix and a work plan.

Draft Evaluation Report: a complete report which will include preliminary findings and possible recommendations will be delivered.

Final Evaluation Report: which will include a full description of verified findings after the review of documentation and data collected, as well as lessons learned and recommendations.

In addition, it should be noted that the report will include the matrix with comments made by the parties.

In some cases, a presentation of the final evaluation to stakeholders is required.

Schedule of Activities

Based on the suggested deliverables and deadlines, create a Gantt Chart with the schedule of activities. (Annex 2)

In some cases, it is required to describe who is responsible for each activity to be carried out.

Finally, indicate the total duration of the consultancy including full name, date and signature.

FINANCIAL PROPOSAL

Before preparing the financial proposal with the breakdown of costs by items, it is very important to consider the number of years of experience of the consultants, the team of professionals in case there is more than one, as well as the average per day paid for similar reviews.

It is also important to consider the percentage of weighting that the proposal will represent when the agency makes a decision regarding the selection of consultants. If the financial proposal represents, for example, 30% in relation to the technical proposal, this means that the agency will give more importance to the methodology than to the daily value to be paid, so one could think that they are more concerned about getting consultants with more experience and suitability and not so much about the amount to be paid.

So, a more experienced consultant will have a margin of some relative freedom to ask for what he considers his work is really worth.

In any case, the final selection will always depend on the number of applicants competing in the process.

Likewise, the selection will depend on the references provided by the consultant and his performance in the interview rounds.

To make the cost breakdown, it is convenient to first check which expenses are covered by the agency and which are not, and then proceed to make a detailed breakdown of the costs to be covered by the consultants according to the unit considered and the currency requested. (Annex 3)

Once the total costs to be covered by the consultants have been calculated, include a payment schedule, which is usually established by the agency itself. (Annex 4)

Finally, indicate the total value of the consultancy in letters including name, date, and signature.

In summary, this book is intended to be nothing more than a simple guide with tips on how to present a good technical and financial proposal for consultants who wish to apply for contracts from international organizations to carry out evaluations of development projects.

ANNEXES:

ANNEX 1:

Evaluation Matrix:

Questions and sub-questions by evaluation criteria	Indicators	Sources of information	Data collection methods / tools
Relevance:			
Coherence:			
Effectiveness:			
Efficiency:			
Sustainability:			
Impact:			

Source: own elaboration.

ANNEX 2:

Schedule of Activities:

Activities	Week 1	Week 2	Week 3	Week 4	Week 5	Week 6	Week 7	Week 8	Week 9	Week 10
Review of Documentation and drafting of the Initial Report										
Approval of Initial Report										
Data Collection										
Drafting of Final Report										
Approval of Draft Final Report										
Drafting of Final Report with comments										
Approval of Final Report.										

Source: own elaboration.

ANNEX 3:

Cost breakdown by item:

Item	Value in Currency
Professional fees	
Transportation tickets	
Accommodation and living expenses	
Life insurance	
Medical insurance	
Miscellaneous expenses (communications, internet, printing of workshop materials, surveys, etc.)	
Total	

Source: own elaboration.

ANNEX 4:

Cost breakdown by deliverables:

Deliverables	Delivery date after contract signature	Percentage of total amount payable	Amount in currency
Product 1: Inception Report			
Product 2: Draft Report			
Product 3: Approved Final Report			
Total payment		100%	

Source: own elaboration.

Gladis María Demarchi

Links to contact the author:

gladis.demarchi@outlook.cl

-october 2021-

Gladis María Demarchi

Printed in Great Britain
by Amazon